The Prophetic Almanac 2023

By
Pastor Bill Jenkins

The Prophetic Almanac 2023

By Pastor Bill Jenkins

 Unless otherwise noted, all scripture quotations are from the King James Version of the Bible.

Manufactured in the
United States of America
ISBN # 979-8-218-10889-2

Cover photo by Efdal Yildiz on Unsplash

Published by
B&B Media
Upland, California
Visit the author's website at:
www.pastorbilljenkins.org

Table of Contents

INTRODUCTION..1

Chapter 1..4

2023 PREVIEW

Chapter 2..12

FUN FACTS ABOUT 2023

Chapter 3..17

2023 VISION

Chapter 4..23

THE BIBLE SPEAKS

Chapter 5..51

PROPHETIC SCRIPTURES FOR 2023

Chapter 6..63

SPIRITUAL FORECAST

Chapter 7..78

CHARACTERISTICS OF 23RD DAY PEOPLE

Chapter 8..84

2023 CALENDAR

Chapter 9..92

JOURNALING FOR JESUS IN 2023

CONCLUSION...100

INTRODUCTION

Every year is different and requires a specific word of God and vision from the Lord to navigate through the nuisances that every new year brings. For over 20 years, I have been releasing specific spiritual insight as every new year unfolds. I base this revelation upon the number that is attached to the year. Every word in the Bible is important, so when a number in scripture is mentioned, it is not there by accident. There is a purpose for numbers. When we do our due diligence and study the pattern of God when these numbers are mentioned, it can reveal the true intent of the Lord for our future. This year we are looking at the number 23. It is only mentioned five times in scripture, so our knowledge is limited when we do a general overview. However, when we begin to look at the chapter 23's in the Bible and the scriptures that have 20:23 in them, along with the individual mentions of the number 23 in scripture, we get a clearer view as to what is to come this year. Also, the most famous psalm in the world is Psalm 23 which also reveals clues as to what our focus as children of God should be in 2023. All of my research is God-inspired and God-led to offer you a vision for this new year.

"Where there is no vision, the people perish: but he that keepeth the law, happy is he." Proverbs 29:18

When a new year begins, it seems like everyone has a thought or insight from the Lord they "feel" they want to share. Many times, it has no biblical basis or foundation; it is just a feeling. It may not be a bad word or even a wrong word, but the church and world are looking for something fresh. In the days we live in, we need more than a parking lot prophecy or some general word that is spoken in the pulpit or pew to encourage people as we enter a new year. I want to give you more than that. I want to give you a vision that you can focus on for 365 days, not just a few days at the beginning of a year. My vision from God is based on the mention of the number 23 in the Bible. This is not an attempt to sanctify numerology, but a genuine effort to search the scriptures to bring glory to God and a revelation to mankind. I am going to give you everything and more than you want to know about the number 23 and its relationship with scripture. Open your heart and mind as I take you on a journey that could quite possibly change your life forever by having you remain conscious of God's vision every day for an entire year. I want you to see 23 in everything and allow it to connect you to the Word of God every time you see it. God has a plan for our lives, so let us pursue a new way of understanding scripture to allow the Lord to renew our passion for Him. Our world is changing by the second and people are turning away from church because of a lack of integrity from its leaders and a staleness in our approach that has turned people off towards God. I am presenting you with a new way to unlock insight from God that will hopefully generate excitement and joy as you connect with God in a new way. Every chapter in this book is another step to closing the gap between you and God. Come dive into the deep end of the pool with me and truly see how wonderful it is to receive revelation from God that is available to all but experienced by only a few. Allow the Lord to show you what to expect from Him and what is expected of you in 2023. Serving God can be fun, and His goal is to set you free to be all you can be in 2023!!!

Chapter 1

2023 Preview

A trailer for a movie is released in advance to create excitement. Trailers do not give you everything you need to know, but they give you enough to help you get an overview of what is to come. Previews are much the same. I am giving you some things and people to watch for in 2023. All of these things are designed to generate enthusiasm and to help you to become more spiritually sensitive. Look for these things in the news and connect them to the vision and Word of God for 2023.

Sports of the Year

NHL Hockey

The National Hockey League allows a maximum of 23 players to be included on their roster.

State of the Year

Maine

Maine is the 23rd state that came into the Union on March 15, 1820

City of the Year

Los Angeles, California

Los Angeles is the 23rd largest city in the world.

Planet of the Year
Venus

Bible Characters of the Year
Women = Jezebel
Men = Jonathan, David's Armorbearer
Youth = Solomon

Bible Story of the Year
The Parable of the Lost Sheep
Matthew 18:10-14

Scripture of the Year

"Whose soever sins ye remit, they are remitted unto them; and whose soever sins ye retain, they are retained." John 20:23

Book of the Bible of the Year
1 Thessalonians

Twenty-three is made up of a two and a three and when they are added together, it equals five. 1 Thessalonians is about being a good sheep or follower of Christ, and it has five chapters.

Fruit of the Spirit
Green Apples

Gift of the Spirit for the Year
Healing

Word of the Year
Shepherd

Color of the Year
Canvas

A canvas is blank. God is giving us the ability to write and rewrite our story in 2023.

Super Food of the Year
Avocado

Vegetable of the Year
Green Bell Peppers

Snack of the Year
Pistachio Nuts

Geographical Places of the Year

- Iran
- Italy
- Wales
- Africa
- North Korea
- Baltic Sea
- Russia
- China

Animal of the Year

Sheep

Sheep are the most mentioned animal in the entire Bible. Approximately 200 times the word sheep is mentioned in scripture. The second most mentioned animal is a goat. So, it is no mystery as to why sheep and goats are often contrasted throughout the Word. Sheep represent followers of Christ, while the goats represent those who are rebellious and choose not to follow the Lord. Sheep were used as sacrificial animals in Exodus 29:39 and symbolically represent God's children in Matthew 25:32. The Word of God even refers to Jesus as the Lamb of God in John 1:29. We can learn a lot about God and His relationship with His children when we study the Shepherd and His sheep.

Characteristics of Sheep

Positives

- Quiet
- Gentle

Negatives

- Indecisive
- Timid

- Excellent sense of smell
- Valuable
- Popular
- Persistent
- Creative
- Submissive
- Great vision
- Playful
- Very social

- No teeth in upper front jaw
- Emotional
- Passive
- Irresponsible
- Wanderers
- Unclean
- Stubborn
- Lazy
- Easily influenced

23 Movies of the Year

1. M3GAN (January)
2. Ant-Man and the Wasp: Quantumania (Feb)
3. Dungeons & Dragons: Honor Among Thieves (March)
4. Shazam! Fury of the Gods (March)
5. Creed III (March)
6. The Super Mario Bros Film (April)
7. Are You There God? It's Me, Margaret (April)
8. The Little Mermaid (May)
9. Fast X (May)
10. Guardians of the Galaxy Vol. 3 (May)
11. Indiana Jones (June)
12. The Flash (June)
13. Transformers: Rise of the Beasts (June)
14. Mission Impossible: Dead Reckoning – Part One (July)
15. Barbie (July)
16. Oppenheimer (July)
17. The Marvels (July)
18. Blue Beetle (August)
19. The Equalizer 3 (September)
20. The Exorcist (October)
21. The Hunger Games: The Ballad of Songbirds and Snakes (November)
22. Aquaman and the Lost Kingdom (December)
23. Wonka (December)

23 Prophetic Dates of the Year

1. Thursday, January 5, 2023
2. Monday, January 23, 2023
3. Sunday, February 5, 2023
4. Thursday, February 23, 2023
5. Sunday, March 5, 2023
6. Thursday, March 23, 2023
7. Wednesday, April 5, 2023
8. Sunday, April 23, 2023
9. Friday, May 5, 2023
10. Tuesday, May 23, 2023
11. Monday, June 5, 2023
12. Friday, June 23, 2023
13. Wednesday, July 5, 2023
14. Sunday, July 23, 2023
15. Saturday, August 5, 2023
16. Wednesday, August 23, 2023
17. Tuesday, September 5, 2023
18. Saturday, September 23, 2023
19. Thursday, October 5, 2023
20. Monday, October 23, 2023
21. Sunday, November 5, 2023
22. Thursday, November 23, 2023
23. Saturday, December 23, 2023

23 People to Watch in 2023

1. Jim Carrey - Actor
2. Russell Crowe - Actor
3. Miley Cyrus - Singer
4. Paul McCartney - Singer
5. Pope Francis - Leader of Catholic Church
6. Harrison Ford - Actor
7. Chris Pratt - Actor
8. Michael Jordan - Basketball Player
9. Kamala Harris - Vice President
10. Ron DeSantis - Florida Governor
11. Volodymyr Zelenskyy - Ukrainian President
12. Bruce Willis - Actor
13. Liz Truss - British Prime Minister
14. LeBron James - NBA Player
15. David Beckham - Soccer Player
16. Vladimir Putin - Russian President
17. George Lucas - Movie Director
18. Sundar Pichai - Google CEO
19. Donald Trump - Former President
20. Max Verstappen - F1 Race Car Driver
21. Kim Kardashian - Influencer
22. Elon Musk - Entrepreneur
23. Kevin McCarthy - Republican Party Leader

Chapter 2

Fun Facts about 2023

Sports

- 23 is the maximum number of players on an NHL roster.
- The youngest golfer to win the Masters, Jack Nicklaus, did so at the age of 23.
- Some sports figures who wore #23 jersey:
  - Michael Jordan
  - Lebron James
  - David Beckham
  - Ryne Sandberg
  - Anthony Davis
  - Marshawn Lynch

General

- In Roman numerals, 23 is written as XXIII.
- The human body has 23 elastic spinal discs between the vertebrae.
- The DNA we have is divided into 23 pairs of chromosomes, and it is precisely the pair 23 that defines the sex of people.
- In telegraphers code 23 means "break the line".
- A 23-sided shape is called an icositrigon or icosikaitrigon.

- State Route 23 is a state highway in California.
- 23 degrees Celsius = 73.4 degrees Fahrenheit.
- W is the 23rd letter of the alphabet.
- The anniversary gift for the 23rd year of marriage is a silver plate.
- The 23rd hour is 11o'clock, one hour before midnight.
- The soft drink Dr Pepper contains a blend of 23 different flavors.
- People who are fascinated with the number 23 call themselves "23rdians"; there is even a Facebook page for them.
- There are 23 letters in the classical Latin alphabet.
- Caesar was stabbed 23 times in Shakespeare's Julius Caesar.
- 23 is the number of the Illuminati.
- Two divided by three = .666.

History

- The first morse code transmission - "What hath God wrought?" - was from the Bible passage Numbers 23:23.
- The earth's axis is tilted at approximately 23°.
- The 23rd president of the United States of America was Benjamin Harrison.

- Maine became the United States of America's 23rd state on March 15, 1820.
- Tola served as a judge of Israel for a total number of 23 years, from 1102 to 1079 B.C. (Judges 10:1 - 2).
- The 23rd Amendment to the United States Constitution extends the right to participate in presidential elections to the District of Columbia.
- There are 23 characters on the face of all the original U.S. coins.

Biblical

- The number 23 is used only five times in the Bible, all in the Old Testament.
- Adam and Eve had 23 daughters according to Josephus, who was a 1st century historian.
- One of the most known and evil women in history – Jezebel – was mentioned 23 times throughout the Bible.
- There are 43 chapters in the Bible with 23 verses in them.
- Words used 23 times in the Bible:
  - choice
  - killeth
  - baptism
  - Jehoahaz
- Only 20 of the 66 books of the Bible have a chapter 23.

- Genesis 1:23 is the 23rd verse of the Bible, "And the evening and the morning were the fifth day." 2 + 3 = 5.

Entertainment

- The number 23 has been the subject of not one but two films: the 1998 German movie, *23*, and *The Number 23*, starring Jim Carrey. Each has a main character obsessed with the number.
- John Forbes Nash, the Nobel Prize-winning economist who was the subject of the film, *A Beautiful Mind*, starring Russell Crowe, was obsessed with 23. The number 23 was featured prominently in his battle with mental illness. His breakdown began when he claimed that a photograph of Pope John XXIII on the cover of Life magazine was in fact him, the proof being that 23 was his favorite number. Nash published 23 scientific articles.
- In the disaster movie, *Airport,* the bomber has seat 23.
- The number of crosses on Calvary at the end of the Monty Python film, *The Life of Brian*, is 23.
- In *Die Hard with A Vengeance*, a train derails in subway station 23.
- In the television series *Lost*, one of the combinations of six numbers that haunts the

characters that they have to put into a computer to avoid an unknown fate, is 23.

- Blink-182's song "What's My Age Again?" includes the lyrics "nobody likes you when you're twenty-three."
- On the cover of The Beatles' 1969 album *Yellow Submarine* the number 23 is displayed on the chest of one of the Blue Meanies.
- "23" is a song by Shakira.
- In *Jeepers Creepers*, the Creeper appears every 23 years for 23 days to feast on human flesh.
- In *The Big Lebowski*, the main characters deliberately use only lane 23 at the bowling alley.
- X-23 is a character in the Marvel Universe. She is named for being the 23rd attempt to create a female genetic twin of Wolverine after attempts to create a male clone failed.
- In *The Matrix Reloaded*, the Architect tells Neo it is of utmost importance to choose 23 people to repopulate Zion.
- "23" is a song by Sam Hunt.
- *23* was a title of an episode on the Will & Grace sitcom in 2003.

Chapter 3

2023 Vision

As we begin a new year it is important to have a vision that can lead us to success. The Bible says in Proverbs 29:18, *"without a vision, the people parish."* As a pastor, I have always loved the beginning of a new year because it is a time for the people to start fresh in their walk with God. I have always provided a vision for the people who want a new beginning by looking at the numbers in the Bible that are attached to the specific year in order to release direction for the children of God. I am not trying to sanctify numerology or give you some new doctrine; I am just taking the Word of God at its word and using it as a form of progressive study to reveal the will of God for a certain year. With the number 23 mentioned only five times in the Bible, I am using not just the specific number 23 but also 20:23 scripture references to reveal a vision for this year. The Lord has also revealed to me the importance of Psalm 23 in developing a vision and understanding His purpose for this year. In many ways this year revolves around the importance of making the Lord our Shepherd. Psalm 23 is definitely the most famous Psalm in the Bible and is the most important chapter in the Bible that is connected to our success in 2023. If we as sheep make the Lord our Shepherd, we shall not want. There will be a lack of things in

2023, but you will not do without anything, if you make the Lord your Shepherd.

Psalm 23

The Lord is my shepherd; I shall not want.

2 He maketh me to lie down in green pastures: he leadeth me beside the still waters.

3 He restoreth my soul: he leadeth me in the paths of righteousness for his name's sake.

4 Yea, though I walk through the valley of the shadow of death, I will fear no evil: for thou art with me; thy rod and thy staff they comfort me.

5 Thou preparest a table before me in the presence of mine enemies: thou anointest my head with oil; my cup runneth over.

6 Surely goodness and mercy shall follow me all the days of my life: and I will dwell in the house of the Lord for ever.

We will not lack:

- Rest, v. 2a
- Peace, v. 2b
- Restoration, v. 3a
- Guidance, v. 3b

- Courage, v. 4a
- Companionship, v. 4b
- Comfort, v. 4c
- Protection, v. 5a
- Power, v. 5b
- Abundance, v. 5c
- God's Presence, v. 6

David wrote Psalm 23 from experience. His first job was as a shepherd and taking care of the sheep. When lions and bears came to attack the helpless sheep, David had to fight for them. David learned the three main jobs of a shepherd are to:

1. Feed the Sheep
2. Lead the Sheep
3. Defend the Sheep

Sheep are not the smartest animals, and they are defenseless against the attack of their enemies. They need to be fed, led, and defended in order to survive.

More Characteristics of Shepherds

- They love sheep
- They understand sheep
- They lead sheep to fresh water
- They direct sheep to greener grass
- They shear the sheep

- They correct and discipline the sheep
- They anoint the sheep to heal injuries
- They provide vision for the sheep
- They show compassion to the sheep

A good shepherd takes good care of the sheep. John 10 is a great chapter in the Bible that gives us insight into the relationship between the shepherd and the sheep. To understand a shepherd's job better, we must understand the sheep.

Characteristics of Sheep

Positive	Negative
- Patient	- Foolish
- Gentle	- Slow learners
- Loving	- Demanding
- Content	- Stubborn
- Trusting	- Curious
- Love direction	- Unpredictable
- Positive	- Restless
- Never miss a feeding time	- Defenseless
- Eat as much as a shepherd will give them	- Dirty

In John 10 we learn that Jesus is the Good Shepherd, and we are His sheep. All the characteristics I have given you of a shepherd match the characteristics of Jesus. All the characteristics I have given you of sheep match the characteristics of the church.

To the degree we allow Jesus to be our Shepherd is to the degree we will experience success in 2023. We must quit putting Jesus on the backburner and stop allowing Him to be an after-thought in our lives. We have proven with our actions and how we spend our time that Jesus is not our Shepherd. We are pridefully attempting and failing to provide guidance and direction for ourselves. We have drifted far from God and the principles of scripture. The worst part is that we are blind to our own spiritual condition. We actually think we love God even though we do not pray, do not read the Word, and do not go to church. We must wake up and open our eyes. We must quit deceiving ourselves and change our ways. The time is short, and the coming of the Lord is soon.

God is calling us to return to Him in 2023 and allow Him to be our Shepherd.

S = Saves
H = Heals
E = Encourages
P = Protects
H = Humbles
E = Enables
R = Restores
D = Delivers

God loves us and wants to save us, heal us, encourage us, protect us, humble us, enable us, restore us, and deliver us. God wants to be our Shepherd. The lines are being drawn, and decisions must be made. This is your time to decide between God, yourself, and the devil. A non-decision for God is a decision for the enemy.

Is the Lord your Shepherd or your hireling? Will you allow Him to lead your life totally and completely, or will you just sort of hire Him for help when you are in need? The decision is yours, and the time is now.

Chapter 4

THE BIBLE SPEAKS

Genesis 23

Changing of the Guard

This is a sad chapter because Sarah, the wife of Abraham and the mother of Isaac, passes away. Sarah was childless until 90 years of age, until God fulfilled His promise to her by giving her a child. Even though she struggled with her barrenness, she ultimately became known as "the mother of nations." She lived to be 127 years of age, but the focus of this chapter is put more on the place of her burial than her death itself. She was born in Hebron but buried in Canaan which at the time was a strange land, but you have to believe that Abraham had a plan all along to obtain land in the Promise Land. Her death represents a changing of the guard, or a passing of the torch, to the next generation. Throughout this year, you will see the ending of one generation and the beginning of a new generation begin to rise up. Whether through sickness, retirement, an inability to govern, or even death, we will see a passing of the torch to the next generation.

CHANGING OF THE GUARD IN 2023

Exodus 23

Honesty is the Best Policy

This is such a wonderfully clear chapter that encourages us to be honest in all of our dealings in this life. Honesty is about being genuine and real. It means to be free from fraud. Honest people are direct, simple, innocent, and uncomplicated. Moses is putting some verbs in his sentences and spelling out the importance of achieving success through integrity.

14 Ways to Display Honesty

1. Do not gossip or slander, v. 1a
2. Do not agree with wrong or wicked people, v. 1b
3. Do not be influenced by peer pressure, v. 2
4. Do not be partial toward a particular group of people, v. 3
5. Do not take what does not belong to you, v. 4
6. Do not ignore other people's losses, v. 5
7. Do not side with those who have been found guilty, v. 6-7
8. Do not accept bribes, v. 8
9. Do not oppress foreigners or strangers, v. 9
10. Do not reap when you are supposed to sow, v. 10-11
11. Do not work when you are supposed to rest, v. 12

12. Do not worship other gods, v. 13
13. Do not forget to celebrate the festivals, v. 14-19
14. Do not be rebellious, v. 20-33

Honest people do not participate in these behaviors. Check yourself, and let God rule your heart. Make all decisions using the scripture as your guide. Never disappoint the Lord by exhibiting selfish and dishonest behavior.

HONESTY IS THE BEST POLICY IN 2023

Leviticus 23

Honor the Feasts of God

Leviticus 23 introduces God's people to the seven feasts of the Lord and their prophetic relationship with the Messiah to come in the New Testament, Jesus Christ.

Seven Feasts of Israel

1. Passover

"Purge out therefore the old leaven, that ye may be a new lump, as ye are unleavened. For even Christ our passover is sacrificed for us:" 1 Corinthians 5:7

Relates to Jesus being the coming Lamb of God to be sacrificed that will cause the wrath of God to pass over those who connect with Christ.

2. Unleavened Bread

"Because thou wilt not leave my soul in hell, neither wilt thou suffer thine Holy One to see corruption." Acts 2:27

Relates to Jesus' sacrifice on the cross which accomplished our salvation and deliverance.

3. First Fruits

"But now is Christ risen from the dead, and become the firstfruits of them that slept." 1 Corinthians 15:20

Relates to the resurrection of Jesus.

4. Pentecost

"And when the day of Pentecost was fully come, they were all with one accord in one place." Acts 2:1

Relates to the birth of the church and the outpouring of the Holy Spirit.

5. Trumpets

"For the Lord himself shall descend from heaven with a shout, with the voice of the archangel, and with the trump of God: and the dead in Christ shall rise first: Then we which are alive and remain shall be caught up together with them in the clouds, to meet the Lord in the air: and so shall we ever be with the Lord." 1 Thessalonians 4:16-17

Relates to the rapture of the church.

6. Day of Atonement

"And this shall be a statute for ever unto you: that in the seventh month, on the tenth day of the month, ye shall afflict your souls, and do no work at all, whether it be one of your own country, or a stranger that sojourneth among you:" Leviticus 16:29

Relates to our ability to be at one with Christ

7. Tabernacles

"Now the Jew's feast of tabernacles was at hand. His brethren therefore said unto him, Depart hence, and go into Judaea, that thy disciples also may see the works that thou

doest. Relates to the millennial reign of Jesus and the Church." John 7:2-3

Relates to the millennial reign of Jesus and the church.

Jesus came to fulfill the law of the Old Testament not to destroy it. Understanding the feasts helps us to gain prophetic insight into the future events of the New Testament and beyond.

HONOR THE FEASTS OF GOD IN 2023

Numbers 23

The Devil Cannot Curse What God has Blessed

As long as we are connected to Christ, we will always come out a winner. The enemy will never be able to usurp the authority of God and curse what He has blessed. Here in Numbers 23, King Balak hired a greedy false prophet by the name of Balaam to curse Israel. Every time Balaam went to pronounce a curse upon Israel to help the king gain an advantage, he ended up speaking a blessing over Israel. Three times he tried and three times he failed. This chapter should be encouraging and comforting to every Christian. God is protecting us from all harm of the devil.

"No weapon that is formed against thee shall prosper; and every tongue that shall rise against thee in judgment thou shalt condemn. This is the heritage of the servants of the Lord, and their righteousness is of me, saith the Lord." Isaiah 54:17

Weapons will be formed, but they will not prosper. The devil will try, but he will fail. As Christians the enemy is always trying to assassinate us by attacking our:

- Finances
- Marriages
- Children
- Cars
- Jobs
- Friends
- Memories
- Homes
- Minds

Anyone who is saved is a target of the enemy. So never allow the devil to discourage you to the point you separate yourself from God. Whatever you go through… God has got this.

THE DEVIL CANNOT CURSE WHAT GOD HAS BLESSED IN 2023

Deuteronomy 23

Cleanliness is Required

The one thing God required more than anything to enter into the congregation, or be in leadership among the people, was cleanliness. Some of these rules were more ceremonial than spiritual, yet they were still rules that were established back in Moses' day.

Instructions for Israel

1. Eunuchs were to be excluded from the congregation
2. Illegitimate children were not allowed to run for civil leadership
3. The Ammonites and Moabites were forbidden to join in religious activities
4. Cleanliness was required for all who wanted to remain inside the camp
5. Asylum was to be given to any foreign slave who escaped imprisonment
6. Prostitution was outlawed
7. No interest was to be charged among families/friends for a monetary loan
8. Keeping your vows was required for access to the congregation
9. Any travelers were allowed to glean from the vineyards

God expects, demands, and commands cleanliness. Not just outwardly, but more importantly inwardly.

CLEANLINESS IS REQUIRED IN 2023

Joshua 23

Be Faithful Until the End

Joshua is giving his final words to Israel in his farewell address. Joshua is old and knows his days are numbered. He cannot give a radio speech or TV interview so he calls the elders, leaders, judges, and officials of Israel to his side one last time and prays these people will spread the news of his last words to the nation. His final words are filled with encouragement to Israel to remain faithful and instruction to always hold fast to the words of the Lord.

Joshua's Final Words

1. Follow the Word of God totally
2. Avoid associations with others who will pull you away from God
3. Obedience to God brings blessing; disobedience brings cursing

These final words of Joshua were simple and straightforward. He was coming to an end of a well-lived life. Joshua was a mighty man of God who was full of integrity and practiced what he preached. He was asking no more of them than what he was willing to give God himself.

BE FAITHFUL UNTIL THE END IN 2023

1 Samuel 23

Have Kingdom Vision

Saul is on a full pursuit of David to kill him here in 1 Samuel 23, and God asks David to help rescue a city while his enemy attempts to kill him. David helps others when he is hurting himself. God often asks us to do tough things to prove our love and show our obedience to Him. David does his job by saving the city of Keilah and narrowly escapes two assassination attempts by Saul. God does not want us to focus in on our enemies and worry about what is going to happen when He gives us a command. God expects obedience!! If we obey God, God will take care of everything else.

> *"But seek ye first the kingdom of God, and his righteousness; and all these things shall be added unto you." Matthew 6:33*

Kingdom vision produces Kingdom provision. Let God take care of enemies. Friends are for comfort, but enemies are for promotion. What would David be without a lion, a bear, seven jealous brothers who tried to hold him back, and a 9-foot giant?

HAVE KINGDOM VISION IN 2023

2 Samuel 23

Appreciate Your Past

This chapter records the last words of David. David was not just a man after God's own heart, he was a man who understood God's heart. He reflects on where he came from, what he went through, what he achieved, and who helped him to accomplish impossible things for God. He is reminiscing about his past and allowing his personal reflection to create a sense of appreciation for everything that happened in his life. David was not perfect. In his last moments with his last words, he could have mentioned all of his regrets, but he chose to focus in on all the rewards that God brought his way. We can never allow our past to dictate our future. We cannot allow our memories of the past to create regret and sorrow. We have to accept the things we have gone through as part of God's overall plan for our lives.

We have to find the good that came out of certain things we went through and learn to be thankful. Take time to look back and truly evaluate your past with your eyes wide open. Give thanks to God and to others who God has sent to help you through life. There are parents, teachers, coaches, friends, family, pastors, and teammates who you need to be thankful for in your past. Look on the bright side and be more positive about your past. Appreciate God and His God-sends!!

APPRECIATE YOUR PAST IN 2023

2 Kings 23

Pray for Politicians

Josiah was one of the most remarkable kings that Judah ever had reign over the country. He lived during an incredibly evil time, yet he was committed to carrying out the commands of God. He heard the pronounced judgment upon Judah from the prophet Jeremiah and was so determined not to allow destruction to come upon the people that he literally read the Word of God to the people of Judah himself. He publicly declared his commitment to God and renewed the covenant of the country to follow God. The people of Judah saw the commitment of the king and responded by willingly following God themselves. Josiah got rid of all articles that were made for Baal and removed all false priests from the sanctuary. Josiah even extended his reformation to Bethel and Samaria. He also reinstated the Passover celebration for the nation. Ultimately Josiah died in battle against the Egyptians, and Jehoahaz illegitimately replaced his father and led the country away from God. The judgment of God fell on the nation as a result of their disobedience, but it was no fault of Josiah. Whether democrat or republican, good or bad, like them or not, the people of God are required to pray for their leaders. Pray for Godly leaders to lead according to the Word of God and not their own personal agendas.

PRAY FOR POLITICIANS IN 2023

1 Chronicles 23

Seek to Serve

David is passing the kingship to his son Solomon. David gathers the leaders of Israel together for the purpose of reorganizing the affairs of the kingdom. He changes the age requirements among Levites for service from age 30 to age 20 because more people need to enlist to serve to make the country run smoother.

The Levites had Four Main Jobs:

1. To take care of all matters within the church
2. To serve in governmental positions
3. To be gate keepers and provide security
4. To serve as worshippers in singing and playing instruments

Levites were servants who understood it is better to give than to receive. If the church is going to be a voice in this world and not an echo, we need more servants to serve. Allow God to increase your desire to serve within your church. The more people that get involved, the more we can build the Kingdom of God in these last of the last days.

SEEK TO SERVE IN 2023

2 Chronicles 23

Renew Your Commitment to God

This is such a great chapter in the Bible that reminds us of, and encourages us that, even though the Devil will always be an enemy to God, he will never usurp the authority of God. All efforts to dethrone God have always and will always fail. Here in 2 Chronicles 23, Athaliah not only lost at her attempt to dethrone the rightfully instituted king, but she lost her life. Jehoiada renewed Israel's commitment to the Lord and re-established authentic worship in the sanctuary of God. This will be a year of many challenges for the children of God, and we can never allow the attacks of the enemy to detour us from God's purpose in our lives. We must stay focused and continue moving forward with Christ. We have to renew the basic commitments we made to the Lord when we first came to a saving knowledge of Jesus Christ.

Renew Your Commitment to:

- Pray
- Read the Word
- Make godly friends
- Be in church
- Put on the whole armor of God
- Think on the right things
- Do good
- Encourage others

It seems simple, but these things work in achieving victory in your everyday life. Evaluate your life and make a decision to go higher and deeper in your walk with God. Remove the bad and replace it with the good so that you can come out on top regardless of what the enemy throws your way.

RENEW YOUR COMMITMENT TO GOD IN 2023

Job 23

Trust When You Do Not Understand

As Job's friends continue their all-out pursuit to attack his character as he is tested in life, Job is falling into a place of desperation where his depression intensifies. Job is feeling lonely and separated from the presence of God. The more he looks, the harder it is to find the Lord. Job confesses that he does not understand everything that God is allowing and declares his need for God to give him a spiritual revelation that might comfort his soul. God gives him that insight in verses 10-12 as Job realizes a few things in spite of his present situation.

Job's Revelation from God

- God has not forgotten him no matter what his friends or flesh is telling him
- God had a purpose in every crisis, and the purpose was not to punish Job but to prove him
- God would one day bring the trial to an end in God's timing, not Job's
- God would bring something good from all the trials that Job had gone through
- God still loved and valued Job because God only attempts to conform those He loves.

When you are going through difficult times that you do not understand, these are hard lessons to learn no matter who you are in life. This year is going to bring heartache and hardships, but we have to trust God. We have to remind ourselves of these wonderful truths that will sustain us through the things that God allows that we do not understand. Do not allow depression and despair to rule your mind and heart in 2023 but allow the Lord to release His comfort through scriptures of promise in your life.

TRUST WHEN YOU DO NOT UNDERSTAND IN 2023

Psalm 23

Jesus is The Good Shepherd

This is a psalm or song of David that is one of the most familiar passages of scripture in the entire Bible. Psalm 23 is used at funerals and weddings to remind us of the protection that God provides His sheep. This Psalm was written by David, who was a former shepherd boy who now was a king operating in the role of a shepherd. David declares the Lord is my Shepherd which speaks to us of a personal relationship with God. David understood God was not a distant deity, but a constant reality to those who allow God to have ownership of their lives. David was confident in declaring that a personal relationship with God brings benefits that are out of this world.

David said when God is your Shepherd you will not lack rest, peace, guidance, companionship, power, or protection. Jesus declares in John 10 on three different occasions that He is the Good Shepherd.

Characteristics of a Good Shepherd

- Loves the sheep enough to lay down His life
- Leads the sheep to greener pastures
- Directs the sheep to fresh waters
- Defends the sheep against enemies
- Anoints the sheep to prevent disease or heal from injury
- Shears the sheep to keep them clean
- Disciplines the sheep when they need correction

Psalm 23 really is one of the most comforting passages of scripture in the entire Bible. Keep it in mind and read it out of your mouth to release encouragement into your life.

JESUS IS THE GOOD SHEPHERD IN 2023

Proverbs 23

Curb Your Appetites

This is such a great chapter in the Bible for us to understand in 2023. When Solomon says in verse 2, "*put a knife to your throat*", this is not a literal translation but a reference to learning to control or curb the fleshly appetites of this world to avoid the bondage that disobedience to God brings.

Solomon's Warnings of Things to Avoid

- Do not be seduced by fame and fortune, v.1
- Do not overeat at the table, v.2-3
- Do not overwork to obtain wealth, v.4-5
- Do not interact with greedy people, v.6-8
- Do not waste words on a fool, v. 9
- Do not steal from others, v. 10-11
- Do not neglect wisdom, v.12
- Do not fail to correct your children, v.13-14
- Do not envy or be jealous of sinners, v.17-18
- Do not hang out with those who will drag you down, v. 19-21
- Do not be a child that brings pain to their parents, v.24-25
- Do not be drawn away by lust and enticed, v.26-28
- Do not engage in behavior that leads to abuse, v. 29-35

Following Solomon's advice is wise and will cause success to come your way. Some of these things may be harder to obey than others, but all of these things must be curbed and controlled in 2023. This year will be tough enough without you engaging in behavior that will only make things worse.

CURB YOUR APPETITES IN 2023

Isaiah 23

Walk in Humility

Isaiah 23 is interesting because it foretells the destruction and restoration of the city of Tyre. The influence of Tyre was both good and bad for Israel. Tyre was a harbor for ships out at sea and a commercial city that was a center for shipping important materials to other parts of the world. King Hiram of Tyre supplied David with lumber to build the temple of 1 Kings 5:1-11. The king also gave Solomon some sailors to help in the labor force for Israel by the sea in 2 Chronicles 8:17-18. However, later it was the city of Tyre that provided one of the greatest threats to the prophetic ministry in the form of Jezebel in 1 Kings 16:31. God promised that the city of Tyre would be destroyed because of its pride. Yet, the Lord declared after 70 years of being penalized by allowing desolation to occur in such a prosperous place that God would once again restore Tyre.

The scriptures tell us that pride is destructive, so we have to walk in humility and never think more of ourselves than we should. If we do not purposely attempt to be humble, the Lord will step in and cause humiliation to be a consequence of our pride.

WALK IN HUMILITY IN 2023

Jeremiah 23

God Loves His Sheep

Jeremiah is giving a warning to the shepherds and a promise to the sheep in this chapter. Jeremiah is telling all unfaithful shepherds that judgement will fall upon them for improper care of God's sheep. Jeremiah was not just referring to actual shepherds in the fields, but also to spiritual shepherds and any person in authority over others. A true shepherd's job is to attend to the needs of those under their authority. God warned that any leader who did not fulfill their responsibility would be personally held accountable by God. God also speaks to Jeremiah to communicate to the sheep, or those under authority, that if they have been mistreated or not attended to properly, that God will heal their wounds, bring increase to their lives, and give them godly leaders who will serve them with a true heart for God. Jeremiah also reminds them that the Good Shepherd is ultimately coming to save them all. Out of the lineage of David will arise a Branch of Righteousness to deliver everyone. Never forget God, the true Shepherd, loves His sheep!!!

GOD LOVES HIS SHEEP IN 2023

Ezekiel 23

Avoid Sexual Sins

This is a symbolic story of two sisters who were the daughters of one woman. Oholah and Oholibah represented the Kingdoms of Israel and Judah. Oholah was the older sister, and her name means, “her own tabernacle.” Oholibah was the younger sister, and her name means, “my tabernacle is in her.” They both were unfaithful to God and were “homewreckers” because they were consumed with committing adultery with as many men as possible. The deception and love of women to entice men will be at an all-time high in 2023. I am not making this a woman problem or a man problem, this is a people problem. Men and women both need to stay in their own lanes and respect their human covenants. Do not be so easily seduced by the lust of the flesh or the lust of the eye. Control your earthly lust and passions. Protect yourself by establishing boundaries with the opposite sex. Do not just avoid evil, avoid the appearance of evil. Sexual sins are running loose in our society, and it is time we quit letting sexual immorality dominate and destroy our culture.

AVOID SEXUAL SINS IN 2023

Matthew 23

Reject Hypocrisy

Jesus is attacking the Pharisees because of their hypocrisy. A hypocrite is someone who puts on a false appearance. They act in a way that is contrary to their beliefs.

Some Sins of The Pharisees

- They expected perfection while not performing their own spiritual duties
- They made others feel guilty
- They did things to be seen by man
- They were greedy and materialistic
- They walked in great pride
- They were insincere in their prayers

- They took advantage of the weak
- They made oaths they did not keep
- They outwardly appeared good, but inwardly they were evil
- They honored the dead prophets, but they tried to murder the living prophets

Wow, what a list! Avoid being a hypocrite. Do not live for Jesus on Sunday and then the devil the rest of the week. Make up your mind and decide whose side you will be on in 2023. The world needs genuine, sincere, transparent, and authentic Christians who may not be perfect but are attempting to get closer to God every day. Reject just going through the motions and make a full commitment to Christ that requires you to be all in for Jesus.

REJECT HYPOCRISY IN 2023

Luke 23

Crucify Your Flesh

In one chapter Jesus is falsely accused, stands trial, is rejected by a thief, hung on a cross, crucified and is laid to rest in a tomb. That is a lot going on in 56 verses. Things in life sometimes happen in bunches and we have to learn to adapt to the changes that life can bring. The key to handling every situation is learning how to crucify our flesh and let Jesus control our entire life. Crucifying our flesh is not killing our flesh, it is denying our flesh the earthly pleasures that cause us to be separated from Christ. It is putting God's will above our own personal will.

"And he said to them all, If any man will come after me, let him deny himself, and take up his cross daily, and follow me." Luke 9:23

"And they that are Christ's have crucified the flesh with the affections and lusts." Galatians 5:24

"I am crucified with Christ: nevertheless I live; yet not I, but Christ liveth in me: and the life which I now live in the flesh I live by the faith of the Son of God, who loved me, and gave himself for me." Galatians 2:20

"Mortify therefore your members which are upon the earth; fornication, uncleanness, inordinate affection, evil concupiscence, and covetousness, which is idolatry:" Colossians 3:5

"Knowing this, that our old man is crucified with him, that the body of sin might be

destroyed, that henceforth we should not serve sin." Romans 6:6

Jesus sacrificed His body, but we have to surrender our hearts to Him. This is a challenging year and at times you will feel you are under severe pressure. Never cave in or give up. It is when you let go and let God that you can finally win the battle. Crucify your flesh and surrender to God knowing the Lord will always have your best interests in mind.

CRUCIFY YOUR FLESH IN 2023

Acts 23

Attack Against the Truth

Make no mistake about it; the absolute truth of the Word of God will be called into question in 2023. In Acts 23, Paul is declaring the truth of God's Word so adamantly that the people are trying to kill him. The truth and truth-declarers will be under severe attack throughout this year. The thing the devil hates the most is truth because it is the truth of God's Word that sets us free.

What is Truth?

- God's Commands, Psalm 119:142

"Thy righteousness is an everlasting righteousness, and thy law is the truth."

- God's Ways, Psalm 86:11

"Teach me thy way, O Lord; I will walk in thy truth: unite my heart to fear thy name."

- God's Son, Ephesians 4:21

"If so be that ye have heard him, and have been taught by him, as the truth is in Jesus:"

- God's Word, 2 Samuel 7:28

"And now, O Lord God, thou art that God, and thy words be true, and thou hast promised this goodness unto thy servant:"

Let all truth be judged by these four criteria in order for any truth to be accepted. Believing what you want to believe leads to destruction. Believing the truth leads to life. Do not allow lies and deception to control you in 2023. Be ruled by the truth. Speak the truth, listen to the truth, and live the truth.

Chapter 23's Summary

Genesis 23	= Changing of the Guard
Exodus 23	= Honesty is the Best Policy
Leviticus 23	= Honor the Feasts of God
Numbers 23	= The Devil Cannot Curse what God has Blessed
Deuteronomy 23	= Cleanliness is Required
Joshua 23	= Be Faithful Until the End
1 Samuel 23	= Have Kingdom Vision
2 Samuel 23	= Appreciate Your Past
2 Kings 23	= Pray for Politicians
1 Chronicles 23	= Seek to Serve
2 Chronicles 23	= Renew Your Commitment
Job 23	= Trust When You Do Not Understand
Psalm 23	= Jesus is the Good Shepherd
Proverbs 23	= Curb Your Appetites
Isaiah 23	= Walk in Humility
Jeremiah 23	= God Loves His Sheep
Ezekiel 23	= Avoid Sexual Sins
Matthew 23	= Reject Hypocrisy
Luke 23	= Crucify Your Flesh
Acts 23	= Attack Against the Truth

Chapter 5

PROPHETIC SCRIPTURES FOR 2023

There are fourteen 20:23 scripture references in the Bible, and all of them give us prophetic insight as to what we can expect in 2023. There is no better way for God to release prophetic insight for our future than through scripture. No matter who gives a prophetic word or what the prophetic word has to say, we always lean on the written Word to confirm the spoken prophetic word. It is only then we have a perfect match. So, here is an idea of what we can expect from God and what God expects of us in 2023.

All Scriptures with a 20:23

LISTENING

"And the Lord spake unto Moses and Aaron in mount Hor, by the coast of the land of Edom, saying," Numbers 20:23

God wants us to listen more and speak less in 2023. God gave us two ears and one mouth, so let us listen twice as much as we speak. We must be attentive listeners to gain all the wisdom that God wants to give us to provide direction for our lives throughout this year.

Commitment

"And ye shall not walk in the manners of the nation, which I cast out before you: for they committed all these things, and therefore I abhorred them." Leviticus 20:23

A commitment is an obligation we are devoted to fulfilling without excuses. Our commitment level must be at an all-time high in 2023. A commitment is a covenant that is lasting, not a contract that can be broken.

Counsel

"(And the children of Israel went up and wept before the Lord until even, and asked counsel of the Lord, saying, Shall I go up again to battle against the children of Benjamin my brother? And the Lord said, Go up against him.)" Judges 20:23

Without counsel, your plans and you will fail in 2023. Make sure you seek wise counsel before all your decisions this year. Wise counsel from wise counselors will help you to avoid pitfalls and instead, experience great success.

AGREEMENT

"And as touching the matter which thou and I have spoken of, behold, the Lord be between thee and me for ever." 1 Samuel 20:23

Agreement releases the power of God in your life. Disagreement blocks all blessing. Walk in agreement with God and others in 2023. Agreeing with God is not going back and forth with God until you reach a compromise, it is accepting what God says without questioning His Word.

LEADERSHIP

"Now Joab was over all the host of Israel: and Benaiah the son of Jehoiada was over the Cherethites and over the Pelethites:" 2 Samuel 20:23

This is the year God is raising up new leaders as He continues to strengthen the leaders who are already in place. There is a fresh anointing on leadership in 2023. As leaders lead others in Christ, God will send true followers to follow.

STRENGTH

"And the servants of the king of Syria said unto him, Their gods are gods of the hills; therefore they were stronger than we; but let us fight against them in the plain, and surely we shall be stronger than they." 1 Kings 20:23

The Lord is providing the kind of strength that sustains through trials and increases the power over the enemy in 2023. Weak people are people who have lost their strength. God is renewing our strength and making us stronger than ever.

DESTRUCTION

"For the children of Ammon and Moab stood up against the inhabitants of mount Seir, utterly to slay and destroy them: and when they had made an end of the inhabitants of Seir, every one helped to destroy another." 2 Chronicles 20:23

Your enemy does not need to be fought in 2023 because your enemy will find a way to their own personal destruction. Destruction is coming to those who oppose the plans of God.

JUDGEMENT

"When he is about to fill his belly, God shall cast the fury of his wrath upon him, and shall rain it upon him while he is eating." Job 20:23

Deserved judgment will fall upon the righteous and unrighteous in 2023. Underserved judgment will never occur in the lives of the righteous. If we judged ourselves, we would never have a reason to be judged by anyone else.

IMBALANCE

"Divers weights are an abomination unto the Lord; and a false balance is not good." Proverbs 20:23

One of your greatest personal goals should be to be more balanced in 2023. Quit tipping the scales and being so heavenly minded that you are no earthly good. Do not compromise, but do not be unbalanced.

Separation

"I lifted up mine hand unto them also in the wilderness, that I would scatter them among the heathen, and disperse them through the countries;" Ezekiel 20:23

Protect your closest relationships and re-embrace your God-sends to hedge yourself against rebellion that scatters friends and separates you from your destiny in 2023. The devil is fighting families and friendships in an unprecedented way throughout this year.

Correction

"And he saith unto them, Ye shall drink indeed of my cup, and be baptized with the baptism that I am baptized with: but to sit on my right hand, and on my left, is not mine to give, but it shall be given to them for whom it is prepared of my Father." Matthew 20:23

Don't run from correction; embrace it. Welcome correction from godly leadership as a heavenly visitor in 2023. No one is above correction, and correction is always a sign of love when it is done correctly.

Deception

"But he perceived their craftiness, and said unto them, Why tempt ye me?" Luke 20:23

If you can be deceived, you will be deceived. Use the Word of God to regulate all your daily decisions to avoid the devil's deception in 2023. All deception includes partial truth, so always check with the Word of God to confirm "truth."

Forgiveness

"Whose soever sins ye remit, they are remitted unto them; and whose soever sins ye retain, they are retained." John 20:23

In many ways you can control your future by the effort you put into yourself to walk in forgiveness. What you withhold will be withheld; whatever you release will be returned in 2023. Forgiveness releases others from their hurtful actions against another and offers grace to the offender. Forgiveness is not about who is right, but what is right.

HOLY GHOST

"Save that the Holy Ghost witnesseth in every city, saying that bonds and afflictions abide me." Acts 20:23

Let the Holy Spirit rule your life. Walk in the Spirit to avoid evil and experience blessing in 2023. It is the job of the Holy Spirit to lead, guide, and direct. Allow Him to do His job in your life.

These fourteen 20:23 scriptures are significant for our success in 2023. I am not just pulling these verses out of a hat; I am attempting to connect scripture with the vision of God. This is going to be like many previous years where good and bad things will constantly be intertwining themselves in our lives. With the help of God, we are going to be fine and come out victorious in 2023!!

Scriptures that Mention the #23

There are only five scriptures that specifically mention the number 23. Although it is a small amount, we still can gain insight as to what is to come in 2023. Every word in scripture is there for a reason, so when a specific number is mentioned, it is not an accident. Trust the Lord that the messages contained within these verses that have the number 23 mentioned have a message for us in 2023. It is really simple and subtle, but these five verses contain a vision for us to be aware of throughout this year.

AUTHORITY

"And he judged Israel twenty and three years, and died, and was buried in Shamir." Judges 10:2

God is increasing the child of God's authority in every area, from the ability to discern, to the power to rule in 2023. Authority is about power and influence. Our ability to influence this world for good through the truth of the Word of God will be at an all-time high. We must seize the opportunity.

VICENARIAN

"Jehoahaz was twenty and three years old when he began to reign; and he reigned three months in Jerusalem. And his mother's name was Hamutal, the daughter of Jeremiah of Libnah." 2 Kings 23:31

A vicenarian is an uncommon and very unused word, but it means someone in their twenties. Look for people in their twenties to experience big victories and rise to the top in 2023. Do not be surprised when younger people experience greater success.

Healing

"And Segub begat Jair, who had three and twenty cities in the land of Gilead." 1 Chronicles 2:22

Gilead was a famous place that was known for a balm that released healing. Look for God's healing power to be released in 2023. This world needs physical, mental, emotional, marital, financial and spiritual healing. Let us allow the Holy Spirit to release God's healing power like never before.

Briefness

"Jehoahaz was twenty and three years old when he began to reign, and he reigned three months in Jerusalem." 2 Chronicles 36:2

It is very possible this is the year where things end prematurely, and peoples' reign over an area is extremely brief. Don't be surprised if things end sooner than expected. Jehoahaz was young when he began his reign, and it only lasted 90 days. Expect the unexpected in 2023.

Blessing

> *"Then were the king's scribes called at that time in the third month, that is, the month Sivan, on the three and twentieth day thereof; and it was written according to all that Mordecai commanded unto the Jews, and to the lieutenants, and the deputies and rulers of the provinces which are from India unto Ethiopia, an hundred twenty and seven provinces, unto every province according to the writing thereof, and unto every people after their language, and to the Jews according to their writing, and according to their language." Esther 8:9*

The story of Esther is a lesson to us of how God uses ordinary people to do extraordinary things. Let God use you to do the extra-ordinary as God does the impossible in 2023. Blessing follows those faithful to God.

These scriptures are a map as to what to expect from God and what God expects from us in 2023.

- Listen more

- Keep commitments
- Seek counsel
- Walk in agreement
- Improve your leadership skills
- Grow stronger in God
- Destruction is coming to those who oppose God
- Judge yourself
- Balance your life
- Protect your relationships
- Receive correction
- Do not be deceived
- Forgive others
- Let the Holy Spirit have complete rule of your heart
- Obey godly authority
- Vicenarians will prosper
- God is releasing His power
- Short-term reigns from those in leadership
- God's extraordinary blessings will overshadow the faithful

Jeremiah 1:9 declares the purest form of prophecy is God putting His Word in our mouth. These scriptures are important to use for discovering God's will and developing a vision for this year. So, lean on the Word of God to release the revelation we need for success in 2023.

Chapter 6

Spiritual Forecast

As always, this year will have many facets of exploration and discovery. There will be good times and bad times. There will be ups and downs. Through it all, we must trust in the Lord that even when things are not going our way, God will work all things out for our good in 2023. God gave me this word for America when I least expected it. It came suddenly and from out of nowhere. This is a sobering Word, but it is given 100% in love from God and me to you. Although this Word is stern, make no mistake about it, God loves you and wants His people to return to Him, so He can be their Shepherd in 2023.

Prophetic Word for 2023

My sheep have gone astray and sought their own way. They have rebelled against My Word and have desired their own will. They have been drawn away by their own lusts and been enticed to believe the lies of the devil. They have gotten so many things out of order that they no longer prioritize Me as their Shepherd. You do not know Me as your Shepherd, and sadly, you do not even want Me as your Shepherd. I am supposed to be first, but many times I do not even get your leftovers. You falsely honor Me with your mouth, but your heart proves you are far from Me. The results are obvious because there is death in your streets, chaos in your homes, divorce in your marriages, upheaval among your children, division among the people, corruption in your politics, wars in the world, and compromise in the church. Evil is everywhere and the innocent are being destroyed. Prophecy is coming to pass before your eyes, yet you ignore what is going on because you have been desensitized by the media. You have sought what you want and what you think is best for yourselves over God's perfect plan for your life. You have sought to build "your" kingdom, not "My" kingdom. You have waxed worse than the people of Sodom and Gomorrah in that you have excused away sin by rationalizing it with the world's philosophy. You have accepted the unacceptable and tolerated the intolerable. You have gradually allowed a transfer of power to take place in your hearts. It is no longer I that rule, but the flesh has taken the reins of power and controls your life. You have very little respect or fear of God in your hearts. I am tired of the rejection from My people. It is I who have given you life and breath. When you are disconnected from your life source you die, although you may think you are living. If a fish needs water and the tree needs the soil to survive, then you need Me in order to have life. I am calling all My people to return to Me and allow Me to be your Shepherd in 2023. No matter what you have done, or how bad it has been, I am offering you a place of refuge; I am offering you a home. I am offering you love, forgiveness, and hope. I am offering you ... your DESTINY!!! I want to be your Shepherd!!! As your Shepherd, I will protect and guard. As your Shepherd, I will guide and provide. As your Shepherd, I will care for you and love you. However, as your Shepherd, I will correct and discipline. I will use the rod of My Word to lead you into righteousness and bring about some changes that will improve your current lives. It will not be easy and will require humility on your behalf. Your hearts must soften, and trust is needed in order to ensure success. You cannot be stubborn and stiff-necked. Allow Me to lead you as your Shepherd so nothing will be for want in your life. I will help you find a place of rest where you will lack nothing. As you seek Me with your whole heart and put Me first, I will give you the desires of your heart. I will not let you down or fail you. As parents protect and provide for their child, you can be certain I will do even more for you than the very best of natural parents. The decision is yours, but I will not always come knocking and seeking your repentive return. Sooner or later, I will take you at your word and get the point that I am not welcome in your lives if you continue to reject Me. My grace is long- lasting, but My soon return is at hand. Time is short and the decision is yours. Take advantage of this moment. Take advantage of this opportunity. Opportunities do not last; they come, and they go. Come unto Me and allow Me to be a Shepherd to My sheep.

RETURN TO ME IN 2023.

Not only has God given me a Word for our nation, but He has also released interesting information concerning the five regions of our country. Use this information to gain revelation as to what God expects of you throughout this year.

In the next few pages, I break down the United States into five regions. Each region has a specific landmark, state, and large city to watch. It will give you a book of the Bible to read from, a prayer to pray, and months to watch closely to see what God is doing. Find where your state is and read the specifics. Keep these in mind as you continue to pray for those things in your region. Journal in the section I provided of anything the Lord shows you correlating with these things or times.

The Five Regions of the United States

Southwest	**Southeast**	**Northeast**	**Midwest**	**West**
Arizona	Alabama	Connecticut	Illinois	Alaska
Arkansas	Florida	Delaware	Indiana	California
Colorado	Georgia	Maine	Iowa	Hawaii
Louisiana	Kentucky	Maryland	Kansas	Idaho
New Mexico	Mississippi	Massachusettes	Michigan	Montana
Oklahoma	North Carolina	New Hampshire	Minnesota	Nevada
Texas	South Carolina	New Jersey	Missouri	Oregon
	Tennessee	New York	Nebraska	Utah
	Virginia	Pennsylvania	North Dakota	Washington
	West Virginia	Rhode Island	Ohio	Wyoming
		Vermont	South Dakota	
			Wisconsin	

Southwest Region

States in the Southwest Region and Their Specific "Word" for 2023:

Arizona – Blessing
Arkansas – Wisdom
Colorado – Meditate
Louisiana – Revelation
New Mexico – Faithfulness
Oklahoma – Power
Texas – Healing

Prayer for the Southwest Region:

The Serenity Prayer by Reinhold Niebuhr

> God grant me the serenity
> To accept the things I cannot change,
> Courage to change the things I can,
> And wisdom to know the difference.
> Living one day at a time,
> Enjoying one moment at a time;
> Accepting hardships as the pathway to peace;
> Taking, as He did, this sinful world
> As it is, not as I would have it;
> Trusting that He will make all things right
> If I surrender to His Will;
> So that I may be reasonably happy in this life
> And supremely happy with Him
> Forever and ever in the next.

Book of the Bible for the Southwest Region:
Joshua

Scripture for the Southwest Region:
Philippians 4:8

Southwest Region Landmark to Watch:
Grand Canyon, Arizona

State in the Southwest Region to Watch:
Oklahoma

Major City in the Southwest Region to Watch:
Dallas, Texas

Key Months for the Southwest Region:
March, April, August, and November

Southeast Region

States in the Southeast Region and Their Specific "Word" for 2023:
Alabama – Prayer
Florida – Deception
Georgia – Obedience
Kentucky – Deliverance
Mississippi – Endurance

North Carolina – Authority
South Carolina – Agreement
Tennessee – Devotion
Virginia – Peace
West Virginia – Faith

Prayer for the Southeast Region:
Prayer By Mother Teresa

> Breathe in me, O Holy Spirit,
> that my thoughts may all be holy.
> Act in me, O Holy Spirit,
> that my work too may be holy
> Draw my heart, O Holy Spirit,
> that I love but what is holy
> Strengthen me, O Holy Spirit,
> to defend all that is holy
> Guide me then, O Holy Spirit,
> that I always may be holy.
> Amen

Book of the Bible for the Southeast Region:
Matthew

Scripture for the Southeast Region:
Isaiah 53:5

Southeast Region Landmark to Watch:
Fort Sumter in Charleston, South Carolina

State in the Southeast Region to Watch:
Tennessee

Major City in the Southeast Region to Watch:
Orlando, Florida

Key Months for the Southeast Region:
January, March, August, and September

Northeast Region

States in the Northeast Region and Their Specific "Word" for 2023:

Connecticut – Contentment
Delaware – Listen
Maine – Courage
Maryland – Rest
Massachusetts – New
New Hampshire – Truth
New Jersey – Endurance
New York – Love
Pennsylvania – Family
Rhode Island – Strength
Vermont – Harvest

Prayer for the Northeast Region:
The Lord's Prayer, Matthew 6:9-13

Our Father who art in heaven,
Hallowed be thy name.
Thy kingdom come,
Thy will be done on earth
as it is in heaven.
Give us this day our daily bread,
And forgive us our debts,
as we forgive our debtors.
And lead us not into temptation,
but deliver us from evil:
For thine is the kingdom,
and the power, and the glory, forever.
Amen.

Book of the Bible for the Northeast Region:
Acts

Scripture for the Northeast Region:
Hebrews 11:6

Northeast Region Landmark to Watch:
Ellis Island in New York City

State in the Northeast Region to Watch:
Pennsylvania

Major City in the Northeast Region to Watch:
Dover, Delaware

Key Months for the Northeast Region:
February, May, July, and December

Midwest Region

States in the Midwest Region and Their Specific "Word" for 2023:

Illinois – Victory
Indiana – Give
Iowa – Salvation
Kansas – Humble
Michigan – Briefness
Minnesota – Learn
Missouri – Inspiration
Nebraska – Life
North Dakota – Forgiveness
Ohio – Correction
South Dakota – Rebuild
Wisconsin – Change

Prayer for the Midwest Region:
An Irish Prayer

> May there always be work
> for your hands to do.
> May your purse always hold
> a coin or two.

May the sun always shine
upon your windowpane.
May a rainbow be certain
to follow each rain.
May the hand of a friend
always be near to you,
and may God fill your heart
with gladness to cheer you.

Book of the Bible for the Midwest Region:
1 Peter

Scripture for the Midwest Region:
John 16:33

Midwest Region Landmark to Watch:
Gateway Arch in St. Louis, Missouri

State in the Midwest Region to Watch:
Minnesota

Major City in the Midwest Region to Watch:
Columbus, Ohio

Key Months for the Midwest Region:
April, June, September, and December

West Region

States in the West Region and Their Specific "Word" for 2023:

Alaska – Protection
California – Trust
Hawaii – Hope
Idaho – Boldness
Montana – Rejoice
Nevada – Unity
Oregon – Temperance
Utah – Grace
Washington – Balance
Wyoming – Work

Prayer for the West Region:
Prayer by Saint Patrick

> Christ with me, Christ before me,
> Christ behind me, Christ in me,
> Christ beneath me, Christ above me,
> Christ on my right, Christ on my left,
> Christ where I lie, Christ where I sit,
> Christ where I arise,
> Christ in the heart of everyone who
> thinks of me, Christ in the mouth
> of everyone who speaks of me,
> Christ in every eye that sees me,
> Christ in every ear that hears me.

Book of the Bible for the West Region:
Psalms

Scripture for the West Region:
Romans 8:28

West Region Landmark to Watch:
Space Needle in Seattle, Washington

State in the West Region to Watch:
Alaska

Major City in the West Region to Watch:
Los Angeles

Key Months for the West Region:
January, April, August, and November

There will be a lot of "head-shaking" going on this year with tons of surprises in store for 2023. We need to pray specifically for our nation, so here is a prayer list for you to follow:

- Pray for the leaders of our nation
- Pray for peace in our streets
- Pray for teachers in our classrooms
- Pray for healing in our land

- Pray for those who protect us in the armed forces
- Pray for the land to bring forth its fruits
- Pray for the bound to be delivered
- Pray for the lost to be saved
- Pray for the sick to be made well
- Pray for the pastors to lead with integrity
- Pray for the weather to be gracious
- Pray for the true godly churches to be full
- Pray for the prisoners that are bound
- Pray for the elderly to be fulfilled
- Pray for the hurting to be restored
- Pray for a fear of God to return to this world

Let us fill our nation with prayer and trust God to release revival in our land

"If my people, which are called by my name, shall humble themselves, and pray, and seek my face, and turn from their wicked ways; then will I hear from heaven, and will forgive their sin, and will heal their land." 2 Chronicles 7:14

Chapter 7

CHARACTERISTICS OF 23RD DAY PEOPLE

If you have a birthday on the 23rd day of any month, then this is a special chapter for you. God is raising up both 23-year-old people and people who were born on the 23rd day of a month in 2023. This is going to be an incredible year for you but stay connected to God. Let nothing separate you from your relationship with the Lord. Be aware of your need to improve your shortcomings and beware of evil disguised as good. Do not let your independent spirit cause you to make decisions that are separate from God's Word.

Stop trying to control things because of your insecurity; instead, trust God more this year. Grow in Christ as your persistence and endurance grows. Hold on and hold out longer than you normally do. Look for ways to be a better giver of your time, talent, and treasure. There are special times of surprises coming your way in 2023, so do not be surprised by surprises or think suspiciously concerning the surprises. Proverbs 3:5-6 is your personal scripture to hold onto in 2023.

"Trust in the Lord with all thine heart; and lean not unto thine own understanding. In all

thy ways acknowledge him, and he shall direct thy paths." Proverbs 3:5-6

Do not fear the future, for God is in control. Let go and let God be in charge. Prioritizing God will help you to be all you can be in 2023.

Character Traits of 23rd Day People

Positive	**Negative**
– Adaptable	– Independent
– Affectionate	– Overly sensitive
– Popular	– Stubborn
– Good communicators	– Impatient
– Clever	– Restless
– Good sense of humor	– Controlling
– Creative	– Critical
– Quick thinkers	– High expectations
– Persistent	– Materialistic

Favorite Color: Green

Best Days: Saturdays

Best Month: May

Scripture: Mark 11:24

"Therefore I say unto you, What things soever ye desire, when ye pray, believe that ye receive them, and ye shall have them."

Keys to Success for 23rd Day People

1. Let stubbornness go
2. Hold on longer than normal
3. Temper your desire for adventure
4. Seek stability

Prayer for 23rd Day People

Lord, I pray for all people that are or will be 23 years of age this year and those born on the 23rd day of any month for You to be their Shepherd in 2023. Lead, guide, and direct them in all their ways. Help them to control their emotions and not be ruled by their feelings. Let their behavior be that of a good sheep who follows orders and not a stubborn goat. Give them favor with God and man in every area of their lives. Release peace and cause them to always look at the cup half-full instead of half-empty. Turn all things for their good and give them the best year of their lives in 2023.

Here are a few famous people that were born on the 23rd of the month:

January

Mariska Hargitay, Actress

Tiffani Thiessen, Actress

John Hancock, Politician

Chelsey "Sully" Sullenberger, Pilot

February
Dakota Fanning, Actress
Emily Blunt, Actress
D'Angelo Russell, Basketball Player
Andrew Wiggins, Basketball Player
Jamal Murray, Basketball Player
Naruhito, Emperor of Japan

March
Kyrie Irving, Basketball Player
Chaka Khan, Singer
Princess Eugenie, Princess
Joan Crawford, Actress
Moses Malone, NBA Player

April
Gigi Hadid, Model
John Cena, Wrestler
William Shakespeare, Playwright
Shirley Temple, Actress
George Lopez, Actor
Valerie Bertinelli, Actress
James Buchanan, US President
Jesse Lee Soffer, Actor

May
Bray Wyatt, Wrestler
Drew Carey, Game Show Host

Joan Collins, Actress
Ken Jennings, Reality Star

June
Jason Mraz, Singer
Randy Jackson, TV Show Host
June Carter Cash, Singer
Clarence Thomas, Supreme Court Justice

July
Daniel Radcliffe, Actor
Marlon Wayans, Actor
Woody Harrelson, Actor

August
Kobe Bryant, Basketball Player
River Phoenix, Actor
Seth Curry, Basketball Player
Gene Kelly, Actor
Rick Springfield, Singer
Barbara Eden, Actress

September
Ray Charles, Singer
Bruce Springsteen, Singer
Mickey Rooney, Actor
Jason Alexander, Actor
Augustus Caesar, Roman Emperor

October
Ryan Reynolds, Actor
Pele, Soccer Player
Weird Al Yankovic, Singer
Nick Bosa, Football Player
Johnny Carson, TV Host
Jim Bunning, Hall of Fame Baseball Pitcher
Ang Lee, Filmmaker

November
Miley Cyrus, Singer
Robin Roberts, TV Show Host
Billy the Kid, Outlaw
Charles "Chuck" Schumer, Politician
Justin Turner, MLB Player

December
Finn Wolfhard, Actor
Jim Harbaugh, Football Coach
Madam C.J. Walker, Entrepreneur
Susan Lucci, Actress
Eddie Vedder, Singer

Chapter 8

2023 Calendar

<u>JANUARY</u>

- National Blood Donor Month
- National Hobby Month
- National Hot Tea Month
- National Slavery and Human Trafficking Prevention Month
- National Soup Month

Jan 1 - New Year's Day
Jan 6 - Epiphany
Jan 16 - Martin Luther King Jr. Day
Jan 22 - Chinese New Year

<u>FEBRUARY</u>

- American Heart Month
- Black History Month
- National Bake for Family Fun Month
- National Hot Breakfast Month
- National Library Lover's Month
- National Snack Food Month

Feb 1 - National Freedom Day
Feb 2 - Groundhog Day
Feb 3 - National Wear Red Day

Feb 4 - Rosa Parks Day
Feb 12 - President Lincoln's Birthday
Feb 12 - Super Bowl
Feb 14 - Valentine's Day
Feb 15 - Susan B. Anthony's Birthday
Feb 20 - Presidents' Day
Feb 21 - Fat Tuesday/Mardi Gras
Feb 22 - Ash Wednesday

MARCH

- Irish American Heritage Month
- Multiple Sclerosis Awareness Month
- National Caffeine Awareness Month
- National Brain Injury Awareness Month
- National Nutrition Month
- Women’s Awareness Month

Mar 2 - Read Across America Day
Mar 3 - Employee Appreciation Day
Mar 6 - Purim
Mar 12 - Daylight Saving Time starts
Mar 17 - St. Patrick's Day
Mar 20 - Spring Begins
Mar 29 - Vietnam War Veterans Day

APRIL

- National Month of Hope
- Distracted Driving Awareness Month

- National Child Abuse Awareness Month
- Keep America Beautiful Month
- National Autism Awareness Month
- National Parkinson Awareness Month
- National Pecan Month
- National Volunteer Month

Apr 2 - Palm Sunday
Apr 5 - Passover (first day)
Apr 6 - Maundy Thursday
Apr 7 - Good Friday
Apr 8 - Holy Saturday
Apr 9 - Easter Sunday
Apr 13 - Passover (last day)
Apr 13 - Thomas Jefferson's Birthday
Apr 17 - Boston Marathon
Apr 18 - Tax Day
Apr 26 - Administrative Professionals Day
Apr 27 - Take your Child to Work Day
Apr 28 - Arbor Day

MAY

- National Dental Care Awareness Month
- National Military Appreciation Month
- National Motorcycle Awareness Month
- Date Your Mate Month
- National Barbecue Month
- National Blood Pressure Month

- National Hamburger Month

May 4 - National Day of Prayer
May 4 - Kent State Shootings Remembrance
May 5 - Cinco de Mayo
May 5 - Kentucky Oaks
May 6 - Kentucky Derby
May 6 - National Nurses Day
May 12 - Military Spouse Appreciation Day
May 14 - Mother's Day
May 15 - Peace Officers Memorial Day
May 18 - Ascension Day
May 20 - Armed Forces Day
May 24 - Emergency Medical Services for Children Day
May 25 - National Missing Children's Day
May 25 - Shavuot
May 28 - Pentecost
May 29 - Memorial Day

JUNE

- Aquarium Month
- Men’s Health Month
- National Fresh Fruit and Vegetables Month
- National Candy Month
- National Great Outdoors Month

Jun 4 - Trinity Sunday
Jun 6 - D-Day

Jun 10 - Belmont Stakes
Jun 14 - Flag Day
Jun 14 - Army Birthday
Jun 17 - Bunker Hill Day
Jun 18 - Father's Day
Jun 19 - Juneteenth
Jun 20 - American Eagle Day
Jun 21 - Summer Begins

JULY

- National Baked Bean Month
- National Cell Phone Courtesy Month
- National Hot Dog Month
- National Ice Cream Month
- National Picnic Month

Jul 4 - Independence Day
Jul 23 - Parents' Day
Jul 27 - Korean War Veterans Armistice Day

AUGUST

- National Wellness Month
- Family Fun Month
- National Eye Exam Month
- National Golf Month
- National Sandwich Month

Aug 4 - Coast Guard Birthday
Aug 7 - Purple Heart Day
Aug 19 - National Aviation Day
Aug 20 - Senior Citizens Day
Aug 26 - Women's Equality Day

SEPTEMBER

- Baby Safety Month
- Classical Music Month
- National Potato Month
- National Preparedness Month
- National Suicide Prevention Month

Sep 4 - Labor Day
Sep 10 - National Grandparents Day
Sep 11 - Patriot Day
Sep 15 - POW/MIA Recognition Day
Sep 15 - Rosh Hashana
Sep 16 - National Clean Up Day
Sep 17 - Constitution Day & Citizenship Day
Sep 18 - Air Force Birthday
Sep 22 - Native Americans' Day
Sep 23 - Fall Begins
Sep 24 - Yom Kippur
Sep 29 - First Day of Sukkot

OCTOBER

- Breast Cancer Awareness Month
- Church Safety and Security Month
- Financial Planning Month
- National Book Month
- National Dessert Month

Oct 2 - Child Health Day
Oct 6 - Last Day of Sukkot
Oct 7 - Simchat Torah
Oct 9 - Columbus Day
Oct 13 - Navy Birthday
Oct 16 - Boss's Day
Oct 21 - Sweetest Day
Oct 31 - Halloween

NOVEMBER

- National Adoption Month
- National Diabetes Month
- National Peanut Butter Lovers Month
- NoSHAVEmber (US – Beard Month)

Nov 1 - All Saints' Day
Nov 2 - All Souls' Day
Nov 5 - Daylight Saving Time Ends
Nov 5 - New York City Marathon
Nov 10 - Marine Corps Birthday
Nov 11 - Veterans Day

Nov 23 - Thanksgiving Day
Nov 24 - Black Friday
Nov 27 - Cyber Monday
Nov 28 - Giving Tuesday

DECEMBER

- AIDS Awareness Month
- National Human Rights Month
- Spiritual Literacy Month

Dec 1 - Rosa Parks Day
Dec 3 - First Sunday of Advent
Dec 7 - Pearl Harbor Remembrance Day
Dec 7 - Chanukah/Hanukkah Begins
Dec 13 - National Guard Birthday
Dec 15 - Last Day of Chanukah/Hanukkah
Dec 21 - Winter Begins
Dec 24 - Christmas Eve
Dec 25 - Christmas Day
Dec 31 - New Year's Eve

Chapter 9

JOURNALING FOR JESUS IN 2023

With all our modern technology, like phones and computers, personal journaling has taken a back seat to other forms of communication. We text and email others, but really have no personal conversations with ourselves. In many ways, journaling is texting and emailing yourself. It is a form of personal journalism where you give an account of day-to-day events in your life. It is a record of experiences, ideas, lessons, thoughts, or reflections kept regularly for private use to help you remember and recall certain things for future use. Journaling has many rewarding benefits:

- It is a great way to unload your emotions on paper instead of people
- It helps your memory, so you do not easily forget important facts and details
- It stimulates your brain and helps it develop a higher level of comprehension
- It helps you to slow down and reflect upon what is really important in your life
- It reduces stress and releases creativity
- It helps you keep track of your ideas, visions, and memories

Journaling is also a biblical principle that is taught in scripture to help us grow closer to Christ as we walk in obedience to His Word.

> *"Thus speaketh the Lord God of Israel, saying, Write thee all the words that I have spoken unto thee in a book." Jeremiah 30:2*
>
> *"And the Lord answered me, and said, Write the vision, and make it plain upon tables, that he may run that readeth it." Habakkuk 2:2*

There is no doubt in my mind that God is calling the church to renew its desire to develop a personal journal in 2023. Whether it is taking notes in church or writing things down that you hear from the Lord in prayer; journaling will help you to show God you are serious about serving Him. Do not just go through the motions, but tangibly do something by taking the time to write and document what God is saying to you. As you document your encounters with the Lord, not only will you be strengthened, but He will be able to trust you more with His Word. You should journal daily, but I have given you 23 prophetic days in 2023 in this chapter to help you begin the process of writing important things down that God is saying and doing on these important dates. Let us put pen to paper and establish a record of all the blessings of God in 2023.

1. Thursday, January 5, 2023

2. Monday, January 23, 2023

3. Sunday, February 5, 2023

4. Thursday, February 23, 2023

5. Sunday, March 5, 2023

6. Thursday, March 23, 2023

7. Wednesday, April 5, 2023

8. Sunday, April 23, 2023

9. Friday, May 5, 2023

10. Tuesday, May 23, 2023

11. Monday, June 5, 2023

12. Friday, June 23, 2023

13. Wednesday, July 5, 2023

14. Sunday, July 23, 2023

15. Saturday, August 5, 2023

16. Wednesday, August 23, 2023

17. Tuesday, September 5, 2023

18. Saturday, September 23, 2023

19. Thursday, October 5, 2023

20. Monday, October 23, 2023

21. Sunday, November 5, 2023

22. Thursday, November 23, 2023

23. Saturday, December 23, 2023

Write out any other dates that may mean something to you:

Date Notes

Write out any other dates that may mean something to you:

Date Notes

CONCLUSION

Regardless of the gas prices or who is in political control in our nation, I am entering 2023 with a sense of hope. All we need to remember throughout this year is that as long as we make *The Lord Our Shepherd, We Shall Not Want.* It is up to us to make a decision to put God first and truly honor Him with our actions. Love is a verb. It requires action. Your words are necessary, but your actions prove your love. You will get out of this year whatever you put in. You can have as much or as little of God as you decide. Every chapter 23 and every mention of the number 23 of the Bible provides a road map for your success. Every 20:23 scripture is your GPS to understanding what you can expect of God and what God expects of you in this year. However, there is no greater way to ensure success than by understanding Psalm 23 and applying its truths to your life.

Psalm 23

The Lord is my shepherd; I shall not want.

2 He maketh me to lie down in green pastures: he leadeth me beside the still waters.

3 He restoreth my soul: he leadeth me in the paths of righteousness for his name's sake.

4 *Yea, though I walk through the valley of the shadow of death, I will fear no evil: for thou art with me; thy rod and thy staff they comfort me.*

5 *Thou preparest a table before me in the presence of mine enemies: thou anointest my head with oil; my cup runneth over.*

6 *Surely goodness and mercy shall follow me all the days of my life: and I will dwell in the house of the Lord for ever.*

Going through the motions and fitting God in when it is convenient for you will not work for your benefit in 2023. God wants to be your Shepherd, not your hireling when you need help. God is not some hired hand you can employ when you are going through trials to fix your situations. He wants to be your SHEPHERD….

S= Saves
H= Heals
E= Encourages
P= Protects
H= Humbles
E= Enables
R= Restores
D= Delivers

God wants to save you, heal you, encourage you, protect you, humble you, enable you, restore you and deliver you in 2023. God's plans are good for you this year, but ultimately you decide who will lead you: yourself, the devil, or Jesus. Make the right choices, and the Good Shepherd will work all things together for your good in 2023. Once the clock strikes midnight on January 1, 2023, this is what you have as far as time to spend wisely:

Months - 12
Days - 365
Weeks - 52 weeks and 1 day

Hours - 8,760
Minutes - 525,600
Seconds - 31,536,00

This chart should open your eyes to make sure you take advantage of the small amount of time you have been given and truly make Jesus your Shepherd in 2023.

LET JESUS BE YOUR SHEPHERD IN 2023

To get daily wisdom nuggets, check out Pastor Bill on social media for the most important minute of your day!

The Minute That Matters

Tik Tok

@pbilljenkins

@pastorbillj

Pastor Bill Jenkins

Pastor Bill Jenkins

Pastor Bill Jenkins

Scan the QR code with your phone, and you will be automatically connected to your choice of social media.

Lightning Source UK Ltd.
Milton Keynes UK
UKHW020806191222
414157UK00015B/911

9 798218 108892